CW01149650

UNIQUELY UNSPECIAL

PATRICIA NWOKO

Patricia Nwoko

Copyright © 2024 Venetian Spider Press™ & Patricia Nwoko
All rights reserved.
ISBN: 979-8-9890481-2-0

Dedication
To Adaeze and Chidera,
who write beauty on the page and raised me to do the same.
To Mrs. Leone
who pushed me out of my comfort zone and into poetry.
To Mr. Leone
who read my words and convinced me they weren't nothing.
To Mrs. Rob
who forced me to be perceived and share my stories.
To my friends, the Katies and Adlers and Graces
who pushed me to write, even when I didn't believe I had anything to say.
To William F. DeVault and Venetian Spider Press
who took a chance on me.
To poets and words and you.

Patricia Nwoko

Table of Contents

AFRICAN AMERICAN 1
    BLACK GIRL VILLANELLE 3
    ROTTEN BUNCH 4
    THREADBARE 6
    SCRAPS OF HISTORY 7
    CITIZENSHIP 8
    THE PROS OF SLAVERY 9
    DOMESTICATION 10
    ANGRY BLACK BITCH 11
    OBSIDIAN SLEEK 12
    BLACK CARD 14
    EXHAUSTED 15
    THE FUTURE 16
    HAIR 17
    RACIST 18
    INNOCENCE 19

AMERICAN WOMAN 21
    SOCIETY CALLS ME 23
    FINGERPRINTS 27
    PERSEPHONE AND INNOCENCE 28
    A RECIPE ON "HOW TO ASK FOR IT" 29
    PAVLOV 30
    WEAK 30
    LOVE 31
    THE ROMAN EMPIRE 32
    PRETTY 34
    IF I LET YOU DEFINE ME 36
    BOARD 37
    SORRY 38
    SURVIVAL INSTINCTS 39
    WOLF WHISTLE 40
    HUNGER 41

AMERICAN TEEN 45
    SMALL TALK AND INTROVERSION: THE ENDLESS WAR 47
    MORGANTOWN'S MARK 48
    MOTH AMONG BUTTERFLIES 52

PRESSURE 53
STAINED.. 54
DEDICATED TO NEXT AUGUST 55
ALIEN 56
AN IDEA OF LOVE 57
REFLECTION.. 58
I IMPLORE YOU TO VENTURE INTO AWKWARD TERRITORY WITH ME 59
ANACONDA 60
A LIST OF THINGS I AM TOO SCARED TO SAY OUT LOUD 61
IMPOSTER 63
FAILURE 64

AMERICAN EXISTENTIALIST 65
ELDERLY ENCOUNTERS... 67
CONDEMNED 68
I'M THINKING OF ENDING THINGS 70
FUNERAL QUANDARIES... 71
TIRED 72
AFTER YOU LEAVE 73
THE EXISTENTIAL DREAD THAT CREEPS IN BEFORE TWO-THIRTY............... 74
DIVINATION.. 74
FOAM SPITTER 75
FOX HOLES.. 76
GHOST STORY 77
I AM THE DARK FILLING THE REFRIGERATOR AND YOU ARE OPENING THE DOOR TO CATCH ME 78
WRONG.. 79

AMERICAN DREAM 81
THE PEOPLE OF CENTRALIA 83
IMMORTALITY.. 84
A LIST OF THINGS MONEY CAN'T BUY 85
A STORY TO TELL YOUR CHILDREN 86
BETTER LIFE 87
PATRIOT 88
SECURITY 89
ARMY BRAT 90
MIDNIGHT OIL 91
THE DAY WE STOPPED RUNNING 92
BLUE MOOSE 93
WHEN THE SUN DOESN'T RISE 94
EUTHANASIA 96

THE AMERICAN DREAM	97
ABOUT THE AUTHOR	**99**

Patricia Nwoko

Introduction

In the Spring 0f 2023, I was fortunate enough to sit on the judging panel that encountered the works of Patricia Nwoko, a young Nigerian-American poet at Morgantown High School in Morgantown West Virginia.

In the inaugural (deep breath) Morgantown High School William F. DeVault Venetian Spider Press Poetry contest, her submission of three poems was incredible. What I and the other judges, Daniel McTaggart (the West Virginia Beat Poet Laureate Emeritus) and John Burroughs (the US National Beat Poet Laureate as well as the Ohio State Beat Poet Laureate Emeritus), agreed on was the quality and maturity of her work.

While not losing focus on her experiences and life as young Black woman, she had a maturity and clarity to her work that well exceeded the pale platitudes of so much modern poetry. It was refreshing and a bit terrifying…while writers and artists can celebrate excellence in a newcomer, there is also a natural instinct to be discomforted by someone with a fraction of your life and artistic experience being advanced beyond where you were at that age. Yeah, I kind of felt like a Neanderthal seeing a modern human walking in and sitting down.

Once we awarded her first prize (which included the publication of this book) and I had seen the contents of this book a few months later, I was gratified and growing at peace with her excellent verse and expression. One always worries about what happens if the manuscript is not up to par with the samples provided, but I was very relieved by the manuscript. Demonstrating a grace and maturity in her expression and presentation, I admit her manuscript was superior to most books that come across my desk. Whether expressing her life as a young woman or reflecting on how perceptions wound her, she is bold, crisp, and resonant.

We at Venetian Spider Press are grateful to get to publish this, her first book, and hope it finds it ways onto the bookshelves and hearts of readers across the nation and around the world.

Respectfully
William F. DeVault
US National Beat Poet Laureate Emeritus

Foreword

As an educator for almost a decade, I've seen many talents come and go in my classes. Some kids are amazing athletes, collecting top-tier college athletic program scholarship offers before their 17th birthdays. Some kids are astoundingly bright and scientifically minded, crafting laboratory-based research projects that college-educated adults couldn't fathom. Then, there are the kids who are naturally gifted in the art of writing — they can craft a story and write it better than you've ever felt it. They string together everyday words to create something extraordinary.

Among these young people, Patricia has stood above the rest and allows me to easily say that she is the most talented person I have ever worked with (and probably ever will). Her keen sense of nuance and ability to craft a poem with thought-provoking and gut-wrenching refrains will keep her poetry relevant for years to come. I have often said that she is the next Amanda Gorman and our country needs her perspective on what it means to be a young black woman in America. Living in Appalachia has given her a perspective that many share but few can articulate in such a simultaneously sad and beautiful way.

In the short amount of time I've had the privilege to work with Patricia (and by work with, I mean that she has shared her poetry with me while immediately exclaiming, "Please do not perceive me!"), she has inspired me to examine my own writing more closely. To have someone so introverted and unassuming write such deeply purposeful and eloquent work is refreshing.

Many students that I have worked with have earned countless accolades, but none more deserving than Patricia Nwoko. I am honored to have been a (however minuscule) part of her journey and I know that the poems in the coming pages will cement her as anything but *Uniquely Unspecial*.

Jessica Robertson
Teacher, Morgantown High School

Uniquely Unspecial

African American

Patricia Nwoko

Black Girl Villanelle

In this movie,
they will whitewash my personality.
Though, I hope that before the credits roll, I will get a happy ending.
I know I am not the main character,
rather they make me the sassy snapping black caricature.
In this movie,
they can't make it a romantic comedy.
I am "incapable" of finding love, lips too big to be kissed properly,
though, I dream that before the credits roll, I will get a happy ending.
I know they will forget about me,
like Chekhov's gun, not useful until the third act has need.
In this movie,
it can't be a horror film.
Truly, my skin isn't light enough to be made of final girl material,
though, I pray that before the credits roll, I will get a happy ending.
I know they will use me,
tokenize and weaponize forbidden words against me.
In this movie,
even when the credits roll, I don't think I get a happy ending.

Rotten Bunch

I am driving home,
the first time you give an apple to me
and, honestly, I don't remember speeding.
This apple is crisp,
his uniform has a trustworthy sheen,
and the experience is sharp, clean
if not for the tang of authority.
When I drive home,
the residue of his warning still clings.

I am stopped on this same dark road
going home.
I bite this apple willingly
with a smile and restless energy.
But his pressed uniform is deceiving
and beneath the flesh
there is something rotting.
Worms take the form of invasive questions
that chew at my skin
and mingle with the mold spores of suspicion.
He holds me hostage in this position
before he lets me drive home
with rot on my tongue and a ticket.

I am talking to my friend
about apples and anxiety.
She tells me her apples have always been friendly,
she doesn't know why I can't shake the taste of
"You're from around here? Really?"
She tells me to get over it,
questions why I chew carefully,
fixated on an apple,
when there are plenty.

Uniquely Unspecial

This other guy,
a friend of someone
who matters enough to be remembered.
His apple tasted like ignorance and gunpowder
and a eulogy.
I heard you put that apple on paid leave,
nestled between the one flavored like prejudice
and a forced apology.
Sometimes your apples scare me.

I am stopped on my way home,
and honestly, I am starting to doubt this is about my driving.
I take the apple,
this time the shine looking more like brutality than bravery,
my hands are sticky with anxiety,
and fear is stuck in my teeth,
and this one is clean
or maybe I just don't know the taste of camaraderie.

I take the drive home slow now
and pray I am never in need.
Because what if the next apple is deceptively sweet?
What if the next apple shoots before he thinks?
What if the next apple fucking kills me?

Threadbare

Maybe I am too foreign.
That's why they choke on my name,
like a needle on cotton,
and somewhere between their throat and tongue tip,
it gets rethreaded.
Lopsided and American.
And somehow,
I learn not to shrug out of my skin like a jacket,
to wear the torn garment I've been given
to feel a little less foreign.

And in its country of origin,
I am the child
playing pretend in a name wholly unfit.
They cannibalize my pronunciation,
chewing at the threads to which it is knit
and somewhere within the strings they find evidence
that it has rejected my ownership
and begrudgingly, they hand me back the pieces,
but never tell me how to reweave it,
and again it is an unfamiliar outfit.

I let my name be tugged,
the strings becoming gnarled and twisted
until it is a whisper of what it should have been
and I am tangled in it.

Sometimes, I wonder if I'm the same girl
even if the name isn't.

Regardless, I hope,
maybe if I adjust the seams just a bit
one of them will accept the way I wear it.

Scraps of History

I'm glad you could think of me,
could scrape off the remnants of your year
and deposit the leftovers you call February.
And, like your faithful dog,
I lap up the stories you give willingly,
choke down the history of "the good ones"
you force feed me
and then I wait patiently for more scraps,
because if history repeats,
if I fight prejudice with peace,
I will get the luxury of your remembering.

Citizenship

When will my mother be so American
that her voice, embalmed in thick accent,
does not revoke her claim to this continent
or provoke degrading interrogation
like she is a lying child
caught with hands reddened by evidence?

Maybe when she can shed her accent
like a snake shedding skin
or scrub the color from her arms
like a stain in linen.
Then they might say her nationality
without the emphasis on the African.
Maybe then, my mother will be American enough
not to have it questioned.

The Pros of Slavery

History is written
with victory,
a white-out
slathered over atrocities.

Where would we be,
without slaughtering natives
and claiming their property?
It's history.

Building something
on the back of slavery
and calling it nothing.
It's history.

Don't let the American Dream
be bogged down by apologies
and empathy.
It's history.

Spare the children's feelings.
No one should feel bad about
the lynching and colonizing.
It's history.

Teach them to smile
in the face of blood-soaked imagery
and smother their empathy.
It's history.

Don't teach them pity,
teach them the pros of slavery.

Domestication

Akin to a beast,
we've been domesticated.

Trapped
in a box of inferiority
compiled of low expectations.
"We only got our place
through pity and blackness."
Compiled of constant patronizing,
because when we are smart
"we are just acting"
rather than being.

Tamed
with subtlety
and small victories,
like arresting our killers
only to set them free.
And having years of progress
only to undo it in another three.
To keep us working hard
and living quietly.

Used
for labor,
a beast to shoulder the burden
of the American Dream.
Laying fields
and voting
for whoever cares
briefly.

Akin to a beast,
self-preservation is obediency.

Angry Black Bitch

I wish I could swallow my tongue
with my adversity,
choke it down
with my voice
and a chaser of animosity—
believe me,
I'm not angry.

But, god,
shouldn't I be angry,
even quietly?
Isn't it owed to me?
To be called reasonable
while I seethe,
not to be made an enemy
for my feelings.
But, of course, I can't
be angry.

Yet, I am boiling,
crackling with rage,
so hot it is burning,
singing my throat,
my vocal cords tearing
with the suppressed screaming
of not being fucking angry.

I just want someone to listen to me,
to take me fucking seriously.
I am sick of being that bitch.
I am sick of my skin dictating my personality.
I want to be more than just
Black
and
Angry.

Obsidian Sleek

It is prettier
to have hair pin straight,
Believe me,
afros don't get first dates,
don't blend well into the crowd
like a good ombre.

They single me out,
scream "black" in my face.
It is better to be
Plain.

It is prettier
not to have a nose like mine,
to breathe softly,
keeping the nostrils in an A line,
not to bring attention
to the mountain piled high.

It singles me out,
screams "freak" in my face.
It is better to be
Plain.

It is prettier
not to have skin like mine.
That will never fit in with the masses,
constantly out of place,
a sore thumb
solely in race.

It singles me out,
screams "ugly" in my face.
It is easier to be
Plain.

I am singled out.
I scream "notice me" in your face.
I am prettier
if boys round here think I'm Plain.

Black Card

Of course I wasn't black.
I didn't chow on fried chicken
and cornbread,
my taste buds had some elevation,
they didn't taste of
no culture and
poor education.

Of course I wasn't black.
I didn't use profanity,
didn't sling slurs
like spit.
Heard for my eloquence,
rather than my loud voice
and big lips.

Of course I wasn't black.
I had a little dignity,
didn't wear bonnets out on the streets
edges always laid,
nails always neat.
You will not catch me
acting crazy.

"You are not like the rest"
was supposed to be a badge worn proudly,
as if my black card
only ever equated inferiority.

Of course I wasn't black
to you.
You refused to believe black
could be like me.

Exhausted

I think I am supposed to fix this ---
The world.
I am supposed to protest,
heart bleeding with the blisters of history.

I think I am supposed to ask
to be seen as a person,
an equivalent,
with education and merit
and black skin,
rather than in spite of it.

I am to commandeer change
in a car constantly running
with a leaking tank
and not to fear dying.
But I am afraid.

I am tired of bleeding
and pretending that history
hasn't made me world-weary.

I am tired of fighting to be seen
by people who view my intelligence
as white washing and affirmative acting.

I can no longer drive a car with a faulty engine
and I am terrified of dying.
But more so,
I am sick of fighting.

Patricia Nwoko

You call me brave as though it's a luxury,
a privilege afforded to me.
As though, in moments of weakness,
I wouldn't scrub my skin
to live this life differently.

Maybe if I had a choice of a better car
I wouldn't drive one steeped in history.

The Future

I wish my belief
in change could span an epic,
yet here's a haiku.

Hair

*It's just hair,
don't be such a bitch.*

Hair
to be grabbed
and tugged
and pulled
and pet.

*It's just hair,
don't be so dramatic.*

Hair
to be observed
and noticed
and ogled
and leered.

It's just hair.
don't touch it.

Mine
to be kept
and cherished
and saved
and protected.

It's just hair,
mine to decide with.

Racist

Racist is a heavy word,
a heavy word riddled with meaning,
meaning to show prejudice,
prejudice now means crossing the street,
the street some thugs are prowling swiftly.
swiftly, you call me a racist.
racist is used so liberally nowadays,
nowadays people speak before they think,
think about how your words affect me,
me? a racist?
racist is a heavy word,
Darky.

Innocence

has always been
White
to you
i think.
and you've always said
White
is pure,
the color of snow
and angels
and pretty things, so
White
babies should obviously matter
more than me,
because the difference between your innocents
and their children has always been pigmenting.
I think you think this isn't black and
White
but, i know
if push came to bomb
who exactly you are saving.
because innocence has always been spelled
W H I T E

Patricia Nwoko

American Woman

Patricia Nwoko

Society Calls Me

When I was 8,
society showed me that I could be unstoppable.
That the world could be mine to command
and the moon mine to capture.
That even if I overshot the moon,
fingertips barely brushing past igneous,
the stars would be there to catch me,
engulfing me in starlight and acceptance.
At 8, I called myself limitless.

And at 9,
they called me *delicate.*
Through eyes instead of tongues,
skimming over my raised hand,
and bypassing the wrist flicking and unconscious bouncing,
Scanning the room for a "strong boy,"
Someone who didn't crack under the pressure of a broken nail.
At 9 years old, they told me I was weak.

But, when I was 10,
they showed me I could be intelligent.
Gave me the taste of an A+
and the rush of that 100%.
Instilled an insatiable curiosity,
only satisfied by answers and worksheets.
Until I knew knowledge,
I did not know I was starving.
At 10, I called myself savvy.

And at 11,
they called me *scandalous*.
Told me that shoulders grabbed eyes
like bait hooked fish,
and math was made difficult
by above-the-knee dresses.
They taught me about spaghetti straps instead of times tables,
lectured me until skirts gave way to sweatpants and camis to cardigans.
At 11 years old, they reduced me down to a *distraction*.

But, when I was 12,
they showed me I could be innocent.
That the "pre" before the "teen" could mean anything,
like Disney movies and theme parks.
Granted me kids' meals
and the feeling of flying high on the swings,
the freedom of almost being something.
At 12, I called myself at ease.

And at 13,
They called me *taboo*.
Told me that pads were meant to be tucked in shirt sleeves,
smuggled in pockets and backpacks.
Told me that my pain was a mockery,
and period, a means of profiting.
"And God don't get so angry, you're just being moody."
At 13 years old, I was just "*pms-ing.*"

But, when I was 14,
they showed me I could be optimistic.
That life could be unburdened by responsibility,
and hands unkissed by calluses.
They showed me I could have friends and dreams.
A life like magazines
and teen beach movies.
Showed me that life was like lemonade on hot days,
savored and shared to ease the enduring.
At 14, I called myself upbeat.

And at 15,
they called me *baby*.
Their whistles like whiplash,
stares like spotlights,
making minutes into miles down empty streets:
adolescence slipped away with every catcall.
Adulthood crashed in with waves of shame I carried home with me in my school bag.
Shame that should have been theirs to carry instead of mine,
shame that should have marked them with humiliation instead of me with memory.
At 15 years old, they called me *honey* and
somehow I was the one left feeling kind of sickly.

But, when I was 16,
they showed me that I could be free.
That keys could jingle like open roads
and cars could smell like new beginnings,
and my future was molded to my fingertips,
and the rest of my life was mine to form—
that I was a touch away from the American dream.
At 16, I called myself liberty.

And at 17,
they called me *female*,
reduced me down to that molecular biology,
stripped me away of that autonomy and humanity
before I even hit 18.
At 17 years old, I became just a body, a *species*.

I am sick of what they call me,
the words they slung to reduce my ability.
The things I am so opposed to.
I am so opposed to what they see,
So opposed to what I know I can be.
I am so much more than just
weak.
So much more than just a
distraction.
So much more than just
moody.
So much more than just
your baby.
I am a million and one more things than
what society has to call me.

Fingerprints

There are bruises on my uterus
in the shape of America's fingerprints

and sometimes they are all i feel
masculine and oppressive
and as the pressure seems to tighten
i am suffocated

and sometimes i forget
i think, for some naive reason,
i get to own this
this part of myself
i am told is the most intimate

there were bruises on me
before i even had independence.

Persephone and Innocence

They steal our daughters.
Pluck them from mother,
whilst their roots still drip innocence,
and call them flowers.
Smother them in the resin
that is the idea of preservation.
Teach them about wrinkles
and aging and ugliness
and hope our daughters cling to youth
because they like the way our girls wear it.

They steal our daughters.
Fresh from their cribs
and crack open their skulls
like pomegranates.
Cram in the ideas of motherhood
and marriage
before our girls have the chance
to learn of anything different.
They hope our daughters cling to this knowledge,
like dew to stems,
so they don't want for independence.

That's the trick,
to steal our daughters
while they are young and defenseless.

A Recipe on "How to Ask for It"

One skirt,
to be hiked up easily.
Can be substituted for jeans,
pajama pants, or leggings.

One low cut shirt,
to show off the breasts.
Substituted for a sports bra
or a turtle neck or sweats.

Two drinks,
for heightened vulnerability.
Substituted for paralysis
or sleep.

A dash of no's,
because ladies never say what they mean.
Substituted for saying "not now"
or saying nothing.

Stir in femininity,
because a lady isn't a lady
if she isn't appealing.

With all these ingredients,
you get what you're asking for.

You ask for it
by not asking.

Pavlov

Boys will be boys
will be a battering ram
against a forming brain
used to make a bitch
learn to flinch,
instead of salivate.

Weak

Weakness comes in the form of pink
and bows and confetti.

Weakness disguises itself as kindness
and emotional maturity.

Weakness is condensed in lip gloss
and face cream.

Weakness is my biggest moral failing.

So as I grow,
and stretch into somebody,

I deny sweet things
and lilies.

I replace pink with
the sleek blue of masculinity.

I abandon dresses
and the notion of being pretty.

Weakness is my own femininity.

Love

The first boy to ever love me
yanked my ponytail,
like a stray thread.

I screamed then,
clutched in his hands,
not knowing this was his declaration.

He dropped me,
thread discarded,
to cope with my rejection.

My teacher explained to me,
after the pain released my head,
that this is the way love manifests.

Love is
the mercy he had
not to pull again.

The Roman Empire

I heard a theory once,
about the Roman Empire
and men's collective thinking.

At the gas station,
I think about the man,
so close,
I taste his cigarette breath.
He leers,
making my body a path
meandered lazily.
Every other gas pump
is empty.

As my tank fills,
I think about true crime
and Exon's bad lighting.
I wonder if the cameras are
watching me
watch the man
watching me.
I hope I remember
how to militarize
my keys.

Hey baby.
I think about lying.
I conjure a husband
Man enough that
cigarette smoke accepts my reasoning.
He glances at my hands,
fingering the gas pump,
as my flesh burns under my safety ring.
He smiles,
yellowed, crooked teeth,
and leaves.

Uniquely Unspecial

I heard a theory once,
that women's roman empire,
is surviving.

Pretty

At least you're pretty,
See
We men,
We break our backs
Breaking into a world
Overcrowded with men like me.
So don't complain
That you can't break in
Lying on your back or
Down on your knees

And sweetheart, you're pretty,
See
We men
We slave away at work
To make money
To make a girl like you happy,
So don't complain
That you have to put out a little
to never pay for a goddamn thing

Because, baby, you're pretty
See
We men
We have to wine and dine,
Pretend we care about the little things,
Remember your birthday,
Our anniversary,
Call you sexy,
So don't complain to me,
That for girls,
Shit don't come easy

Uniquely Unspecial

You think I'm pretty?
That's exactly what I need,
To be called hot
instead of witty,

To be plied with drinks
To get me ready for the plowing,
To be reduced to tits and a tight ass
When I want to be taken seriously,
Thank god I'm fucking pretty.

If I Let You Define Me

I'd probably be
bossy[1]
because "assertive" would fit a little too much like
daddy's suit jacket.
Or, maybe
ambitious[2]
because "determined" is reserved for CEOs,
not girls in their first high-ranking positions.
Or, likely
emotional[3]
because tears have been known to be more
destructive than fists.

If I let you define me,
I think my description would be
Woman[4] .

---

[1] *Adjective*
　　meaning "Who does this bitch think she is?"

[2] *Adjective*
　　meaning "Cute to think she'd ever have her own office."

[3] *Adjective*
　　meaning "Better watch out, she's on her period"

[4] *Noun*
　　"lesser than"

Board

There is a board of men
unraveling
my education
to mere ribbons
to be retied,
until my thoughts work the way
they want it

they tell me i'd look prettier
uneducated

There is a court of men
dissecting my body into
amendments
placing me neatly
into their constitution,
dismembered
until I fit

they tell me i'd look prettier
with a fetus

There is an association of men
Ripping holes into
my security
with gunshots
and decisions colored with
self-interest
Trading my safety for an AK-47

they tell me i'd look prettier
as a patriot

Sorry

It starts with sorry,
this stripping of authority.

It is a sorry stuck in her teeth,
tinging her words with the stench
of unsurety
disguised as an apology.

It is a sorry sometimes spoken
and sometimes it is the silence
after interrupted speech
and sometimes it is stepping to the right
As authority trudges down the center
unwavering.

It is a sorry
they use to keep her submissive
the little ways they make her apologize
for existing.

Survival Instincts

to survive
your body
rewires release,
makes his grunting, bruising speed
easy
makes his crushing, suffocating weight finish
quickly
makes this pain possible for
surviving.

to survive
your brain
rewrites history,
makes that feeling, trapped and helpless, a
memory
makes the trauma tearing through your legs a
dream,
makes this pain possible for
surviving.

to survive,
you
redefine security,
make choices that cannot be deemed
risky
make enough room between you and men for
safety
make your pain possible for
surviving.

in times like these, you rely on
survival instincts.

Wolf Whistle

I kind of like catcalls,
in the *oh my god is he gonna kill me?*
kind of way,
in the *oh my god is he gonna kill **me**?*
kind of way.
In the way that I have learned to
exchange my self-worth for a man's idea of my beauty
and derive a little validation
from the "nice tits sweetie,"
he calls from his car.
And of course it's degrading,
but, I mean, he thinks I'm pretty.
And I'm pretty sure it's pathetic
to want this random man to want me.
But, name a better way of valuing yourself
in this society.
I think I kind of like catcalls,
in a woman kind of way,
if you get what I mean.

Hunger

I am so hungry,
starving for food and knowledge
and the perfect body,
and I have found you are not allowed
to be full
of all three things.
I have learned how to pick my priorities.
How to stop my body from shutting down
with just a cube of cheese.
How many squats and push-ups and planks
are needed to make the girl in the reflection worthy
of a scrap of something,
that something being the three numbers on a scale,
low enough to let her sleep.
How many minutes in a mile
until her stomach screams.
I have learned from watching and listening and learning
that food is the only resource
in which you want to be starving.

Men Must Be Gods

To have the audacity of a man
is to be a God, I think.
It is demanding someone kneel before you
and then beg for your mercy
when they have never liked it much on their knees.
Because loving men and Gods
begets suffering.
And I have only known a God to be as unrelenting
as a man can be.
But, then again, what else is a man
if not the liberator
to the victims of his tormenting.
This ability men have,
to turn someone subservient and wanting,
to detach themselves from our humanity
must be holy.
Because I, as a human being,
could not do to another,
what a man has done to me.

Romance

Being loved by men
will always feel like coercion.
Because all great love stories begin when he asks
again
and she relents.
And sure, it is dressed up
in showy romantic gestures and roses.
But, in the end,
it is always a chase and acquiescence
and the knowledge that he will always make her say yes.

Patricia Nwoko

American Teen

Patricia Nwoko

Small Talk and Introversion: The Endless War

Small talk and I are adversaries,
constantly we battle and constantly I bleed,
pieces of myself pouring into casual conversation,
like blood from a dismembering.
I pray for this to cease.

I abandoned the pieces of me, casualties of war,
and yet I hold requiem,
late at night, when distractions fail and thoughts run rampant.
Sometimes, I wonder how much of myself I have left,
not flowing unthinkingly or willingly ignored,
but wholly mine.
I beg for this to cease.

Is it the reason my reflection remains incomplete,
holes burrowed in places that once held flesh and memory.
Maybe my deficit is caused by the fragments I surrender
to strangers in the gift bags I call goodbyes.
Maybe it's why I'm doomed to crave validation and completion,
like Tantalus craves food and water.
Always in reach, but never reachable.
When will it cease?

This is my punishment.
For my inadequacy or for my complacency,
only you know.
I am trapped in your cycle, always yearning and always giving.
Will it ever cease?

Often, in times like these, I wish to be put out of my misery,
left mute, but complete.
I mull over which came first,
the pieces handed freely,
or the pieces mourned and missing.
Cease fire, please?

Patricia Nwoko

Morgantown's Mark

I used to hate telling people where I was from.
The syllables of my city painted ugly inaccuracies.
I knew if I told them, they would give me their opinion,
unwarranted, unoriginal, and mean,
bashing my hometown
before the letters had even left my lips fully.

They tell me I am from college kids,
from the acrid smoke of fabric couches
burned to a crisp
and backed up traffic.
From alcohol poisoning
and drunk students,
children barely eighteen dying in frat houses.
From a college
losing programs
and letting down its residents.

They tell me I am from education,
yet I am faced with the ignorance.
Libraries stripped by congress
and going desolate.
Yards adorned with flags
to commemorate the Confederates,
as if this state wasn't created for a reason.
Bibles and words used like bullets and rifles
as deadly weapons.

They tell me I am from opiates,
from the highways carrying something deadly
into the mountains
From families stuck in a cycle
pills popping into poverty
and eventually addiction.
They tell me death and our state name
Have become synonymous.

Uniquely Unspecial

They tell me I am not Appalachian,
but rather from the city.
They tell me these hands are free
of coal dust
and mine accident fatalities.
They tell me we are soft and we are weak
and this city isn't worth including

But, I know the facts,
know the statistics
Believe me.
But, I know they aren't really looking,
not at the good things,
not past the search engines and history,
If they were,
Their conclusions and ending wouldn't be so different
from my roots and beginnings.

Because I am from game days,
a sea of gold and blue flowing up downtown streets,
and a feeling of good company.
I am from the call and response of strangers,
From Let's go Mountaineers
and a W and a V.
I am from a team with a losing streak
that still has full stadiums
with fans always cheering.

Patricia Nwoko

I am from memories.
From the Morgantown Public Library,
the ache of carrying too many books
and the dusty smell of a good story.
From Miller's laundromat trips,
stockpiled with coin changer quarters
and snacks from the vending machine.
From neighbors,
block parties stuffed with pepperoni rolls
and scented with fire crackers and sunscreen.

I am from nature
From all four seasons,
from the snow I pretend to hate,
and budding flowers and fallen leaves.
I am from cooper's rock
and rail trails and hikes
and rocks forming.
I am from beauty
from the Mon and sugar maples
and rhododendrons and trees.

I am from art,
From Harriet Tubman painted on a brick building
and tiny, little paintings scattered across the city.
From the moonlight market,
filled with handcrafted necklaces
and teenage friendships and found families.
From blue moose,
where spoken word and music
flow like coffee.

Uniquely Unspecial

I am from a community.
I am from generations,
people falling in love and having babies,
planting their legacies like seeds.
I am from culture and rivalries
from sweet caroline and Pitt hating,
and mothmen and mythology.
I am from volunteering
children helping children
and families helping families.

I am from wild and wonderful,
I am from gold and blue,
I am from country roads and mountains.
I am from WVU
I am from Morgantown, West by God Virginia,
and this is not for them,
No this is for me and you.

Moth Among Butterflies

There's a moth among butterflies.
Grouped here, around this bloom and these petals,
Sipping sweet nectar from its proboscis
And dancing in these rays of sunlight,
You almost wouldn't know it,
Ethereal in its camouflage.

Yet, there is a moth among butterflies.
Maybe it is something to do with the way it's ostracized.
Pushed to the edges of the gardens,
Dulled wings made friendly with the wind.
There is something so telling about it,
Embarrassing in its visibility.

Just a moth among butterflies.
Perched delicately on the edges of companionship,
Longing to close the distance created
By evolution and self-preservation,
Longing for the days before
They were a moth among butterflies
And a butterfly among moths.

Pressure

I was not mined,
Not axed through caves,
but crafted carefully from calcium.
And yet you apply expectations and pressure
Like I am a piece of coal,
Won through hard labor
Instead of a work of cartilage.

That same pressure
Snaps bones instead of shining them.
And still you wonder why I am broken,
As if I owed you accomplishments.

After enough pressure and enough time,
I too understand your disappointment
I too compare my fractures to diamonds
I too wonder why I only ever splinter
Instead of shining.

Stained

My inferiority is like a stain cleaned
self-deprecation and pink
sink into the fibers of my soul
and are scrubbed raw
until there is only a memory of ink
that has consumed my being.

Dedicated to Next August

We cling to the brick like wallflowers,
petals peering through
stalks of passing legs to watch the game
and there is something sparking in the cooling air.

Firsts and lasts
and last firsts.
And this is the last first time I will cling to this wall.

There was a time I was a seed,
planted here,
and now I am a bursting bloom,
watching seeds feed on Friday Night Lights.

Next year,
a seed will replace me.
And feed on Zuls and friendship
and lack of football knowledge
like photosynthesis.

They, too, will stomp on bleachers,
and throw baby powder,
and wear school colors.

They, too, will be planted here,
on my wall,
and bloom over the years
to become a beautiful something.
To become a wallflower reminiscing.

Alien

There is an alien in this skin.
Flesh pulled taut over uncomfortable bones
and gums tight against awkward teeth.
This alien cannot smile
with human quality.

There is an alien in this skin.
Tongue twisted sloppily
with poor sentence grouping.
This alien can not speak without
pregnant pauses and choppy stuttering.

There is an alien in this skin.
Food mashed too quickly
and feet moving with too much speed.
This alien can not function
without choking and tripping.

There is an alien in this school.
And people are staring
and its skin is bubbling and boiling.
This alien can not be seen
without the body cooking beneath.

Social anxiety
has made an alien out of me

An Idea of Love

Love, I think,
is warm rain
after a dry summer

When you fear
you will fall into autumn's chill embrace
without the kiss of summer's raindrops.

And then,
as the sun beats by
in the dwindling heat.

Rain

Sprinkles falling into sheets,
hugging tightly
until you forget everything.

Life and responsibility
and the emptiness of summer
and being lonely.

A good summer rain
feels a little like
love

I think.

Patricia Nwoko

Reflection

Refracted
night distorts
face
into pieces,
reconstructing
something *bigger,*
inches
antagonized over
with
something *odder,*
ugly.
Nose askew,
crooked,
eyes uneven.
Clown
glares back.
A
bathroom mirror
turned
funhouse attraction.

I Implore You To Venture Into Awkward Territory With Me

To sit in uncomfortable facetime silence with me,
exchange awkward smiles as currency
and indulge on the empty pauses like delicacies,
devoid of substance and meat

Come be consumed by first dates,
swallow stilted small talk and focus on the other's face,
as if there is nothing more interesting
than your freckles out of place.

Let me feast on the mundane,
tell me your favorite color so I can digest
yellow and useless moments
and discuss interests and our feelings on fate.

I implore you to venture into awkward territory with me
so we can maybe become anything.

Anaconda

There is an anaconda that lives in my chest.
One that's formed a river from my veins.
A rainforest from my ribs.
And sometimes It coils around my heart
And clutches on my anxious afib
And It squeezes,

its thick skin making my lungs claustrophobic
crowding them into my ribs
so my breath is constricted
caught between predator
and where it is headed
and then the pressure rises
as i begin to question
how much longer i can breathe out
without breathing in
there is so much pressure
i can hear it squeezing on my organs
so much pressure
my chest should cave in
killing me
and crushing it
in the face of my panic
the harder it squeezes
and i am seconds from
surrendering to it

And suddenly I can breathe again
And It slithers back into my blood
To sit.

There, my anxiety waits
for its next moment.

A List of Things I am Too Scared to Say Out Loud

i am scared of the dark,
and the things it is hiding

like monsters and enemies

i am worried about the amount that i worry
and i worry I am wrong about everything,

like social interaction and feelings

i am glad that you are gone
almost as sad as I am about your going

i wish you could have loved me

i am sorry to everybody who has ever met me
and i am constantly sorry

please forgive me

i am embarrassed about the little things,
like walking through hallways

and crying

i wish someone would have talked to me,
anyone really

living in my brain gets lonely

i think everyone hates me,
or maybe is just polite in their loving

(maybe I hate me)

Patricia Nwoko

i wish saying things out loud was easy
and i worry paper might be the only thing to get me

this poem akin to therapy

i am scared i will invite you into my exposed skeleton,
and you will leave.

Imposter

A changeling
has stolen the person meant to be here
and replaced them with me
(or rather, I am the changeling)
A changeling (me)
has stolen the person (someone more important or with more experience or more everything)
and has replaced them (selfishly) with me (the changeling)
So I am sorry,
but I can not do this
(or rather, I am sorry, so I can not do this)
I (a changeling) have empathy,
enough to know that I can not do this (to you or me)
But maybe they will come back,
maybe you will find someone better
than me (the changeling)

Patricia Nwoko

Failure

is a b,
second semester,
and a 3.95 unweighted

and it is a missed pass,
on a crowded field
when we are down by ten,

and it is a poem
written by someone
too scared to call herself a poet

and a dream of being a writer
and a stutter
with a couple stunted sentences

and an unresolved friendship
and a bad outfit
and an unread text

failure is this brain,
a failure is writing this,
a failure is leaving this unfinished

American Existentialist

Patricia Nwoko

Elderly Encounters

There is an old man on this bus,
sitting in a seat and a memory
and he is rambling.
A scattered love story
blows past me like loose leaves
and piles into an idea of a lovely history
and as I wait for my stop,
I listen intently.

There is an old woman in this Walmart,
her cart overflowing with necessities
and yet she stops to talk to me.
Her childhood grows in front of me,
like the garden her mother was always tending,
and she waters the roots
of a lifetime and red hair, since fading.
For a couple moments,
I am ensnared in this woman I will never again meet.
and when I get home,
I have brought back more than groceries.

There will be an old woman in this mirror before me.
I wonder if she will be lonely.
If she will miss the color of her hair
or her drifting memory.
Or if she will have countless stages
and countless audiences to keep her company
To reminiscence in bus seats and over groceries.

Condemned

I fear God has turned away from me.
I wonder how long it's been
since I began memorizing the contours of his back,
the way the slopes in his muscles spell out disappointment
instead of guidance.
The way his silence deafens my confessionals
instead of bolstering my hymns.

I fear God has turned away from me,
and yet, the devil still stands.
He stares unwavering into the mess of sin I am becoming,
the pride and greed and envy threaded into the fiber of my being.
He does not get angry
at what he is creating
and, I have yet to meet his charred and mottled wings,
so what is the harm in falling?

I fear God has turned away from me
because I can't mold myself into something he can love,
because my form was made to shift
and take foundational change
a part of me craves to be wanted,
not ironed out and holy
and despite my flaws, the devil still wants me,
he is unafraid to love where you hate.

I fear God has turned away from me
and maybe not wanting to be holy
has him running.
Maybe, my eyes straying towards the devil's
is like a spotlight burning over my weakness,
an acknowledgement that I am not strong,
and maybe I was not created in the image of strength.

Uniquely Unspecial

I fear God has turned away from me
and I am uncertain I can keep praying to a faceless being,
I am tired of kneeling to someone who will not acknowledge me
of bruises on my spirit and my knees
Once, likely the day of reckoning,
he will finally deign to face me
and I will no longer be waiting.

Patricia Nwoko

I'm Thinking of Ending Things

On the edge of a staircase,
my feet sinking in wet concrete,
I debate jumping.

I imagine my head cracked open,
blood flooding through cracks
and brain matter congealing next to me.

I step instead of leap.

I'm thinking of ending things,

In biology,
I contemplate mourning,
those who will miss me,
how the clouds will keep on drifting.

I imagine Earth orbiting,
circling the sun,
as thoughts circle my memory.

I am back to note-taking.

I'm thinking of ending things

Over lunch,
I wonder if they can see it,
an x-ray
burning through skin and brave face.

And maybe it's conceited
to think that anyone spends their precious moments on me,
to think I'm worthy of passive considering

    I go back to eating

    and thinking about ending things.

Funeral Quandaries

After you are gone,
they offer up condolences,
prayers to a false altar
of a man they reimagine
to be worth remembering.

And I am made heavy,
by carrying their idea of grief
alongside my own memory.

I know not what to do with the consoling.

Lay them at your grave?
Lies to be replayed eternally,
of a man,
better than the one laid
six-feet deep.

Keep them?
Attempt to mend my heart's cracked lining,
with the bandages of pretending.

I know not how to grieve.

To mourn
while weighed down
by false memory,
of an angel
you never had the chance to be.

To bemoan a man,
I no longer trust myself
remembering.

Tired

I will get no sleep
tonight.
I will think of the children
bombed in their beds,
smothered by smoke,
while I sink into satin.
I will think of the families
cut at clutched fingertips
and ripped ragged.
No dreams materialize
from their scattered remnants.

I will get no sleep
tomorrow.
I will tune out the screams like static,
cover them with avoidance
and television.
I will let myself forget.
Bury my compassion
like they bury their dead.

I think
I will get no sleep
In the end.

after you leave

i
unravel

after the news
when i feel nothing
but the splinters of words and
condolences

after the funeral
when you are laid low
to live amongst dirt and eternity

after the eulogy
where I hear you as they speak

in the silence

and your absence

and the peace

i

unravel

completely

The Existential Dread That Creeps In Before Two-Thirty

It is two am
and I am
rethinking my existence,
clock ticking
towards three
hurtling me
towards the impossibility
of infinite possibilities
drowning me in the minutes
of two-sixteen

Divination

Maybe the gods are like us.

Maybe they flock to validation
like sinners to the altar.
We validate our lives with
others compliments
the way they validate their existence
with our attention.

Maybe they too don't know
their strengths
the way they are consumed by
weakness,

Maybe we are like the gods
when it comes to craving worship.

Foam Spitter

the morning after
fifty sleeping pills
sunk into my stomach lining
like stones in a creek

i woke up

with a stomach ache and surprise
weighed down to the earth
with lead in my center
and cement on my feet

so close to hell
i could feel the crust of the earth
caving in under me
bubbling with heat

it should have killed me
i think
cause i was craving something deadly
at three am and i was lonely

i should be angry it didn't
kill me
that the stones i swallowed
didn't drag me into an early grave
and eternal sleep

the morning after
i swallowed fifty pills
i woke up
and that made me surprisingly

Happy

Patricia Nwoko

Fox Holes

There are no atheists in foxholes
they tell me.

Your faith is hammered in
by the bullet holes,
making corpses of mothers' children.

They tell me it is those moments,
eye to eye with death,
where you ask God for forgiveness.

Yet, there were no prayers to the officer
who stood like death
darkening my doorstep.

Faith fled fast,
grief lingered in the void left
as the officer retreated.

You won't find them in foxholes,
because funerals attract the most atheists.

Ghost Story

It must be so lonely.
To be anchored here
by matter and memory,
holding so tight
to your recollection
of existing

cabinets shake
and wind whispers
and you cross over mortality
to be seen.

Please

haunt me
with your yearning,
pull me
into your company,

make me
a character
in the ghost story
that will mark
your eternity.

Patricia Nwoko

I Am The Dark Filling The Refrigerator and You are Opening the Door to Catch Me

and we are engaging in a game of chicken
to see how quickly i can move
so as not to be perceived.
you think that you are winning.
you cite the glimpses you catch before the light comes in
to save me
as evidence i am warming to this visibility.
you think, maybe, i am staying longer between the fridge door and the light,
just for your viewing.
i am not.
and as you stretch the scraps of me into an eternity
i am getting faster at leaving
and one day, likely,
you will open up this door
and there will only be light
and i will have escaped
being seen.

Wrong

There is a shard of something broken
lodged in my esophagus
and sometimes I want to reach my hand into
the cavernous empty that is my stomach
and pluck it,
yank until the blood and pain and strange pour out of me
or maybe surgery will pull it up and out the yawning empty.
Sometimes I try to extract it with a paper and a pen,
and I think maybe it is coming loose,
maybe the strange has funneled free,
and I stop and yet
I am still a vessel to a foreign being.

Maybe I will always have this strange lodged in my body.
Maybe I was never made for normalcy.

Patricia Nwoko

American Dream

Patricia Nwoko

The People of Centralia

are smudged with the smoke of your sins,

they think,
the people of centralia,
that maybe you are the fire
warm under their feet,
lapping up the walls of their homes
the way you lap up your money,

they think you are the flame
burning blisters onto their skin
and hissing against their heels
on the ever warm ground,

the people of centralia
are wrong,

somehow you are worse than the fire
turning memories to embers,
you are the smoke
insidiously sweeping up chimneys
and choking out the lungs of centralia

and on the wind
you get to leave,
these are not your homes
you have left burning

singed at the expense
of your greed.

Immortality

As I lay,
smothered by the sheets
that will be my eternity,
you tell me a story about
immortality.

About the vampires
made from drawings on a page,
multi-colored shadows
making moments eternally.

About eternal beings
and the way gods are made
by a chisel and stone
and a couple decades.

About me,
the way my soul has scattered
among these stanzas
and these words
hold my heart beat.

On my deathbed,
before I get to sleep,
you tell me that this
will be my immortality.

A List of Things Money Can't Buy

Money can't buy happiness
or the heights stitched into door frames
with tip-toes and sharpie.
Money can't buy the notches wedged into the flooring
knocked there by half a dozen siblings
or the memory
layered between paint and concrete.

Money can't buy angst
or the sound of anger crashing against hinges
and the slam of a door
or the taste of an argument
served with mama's fine china and green beans.
Money can't buy the pride hung haphazardly
with a magnet and an acceptance letter and victory.

Money can't buy everything.
Or maybe, I am confused.
Maybe *someone's* money can buy anything,
Maybe it has already,
Maybe that's why I can't buy happiness
or angst
or my childhood home
on my own salary.

Patricia Nwoko

A Story To Tell Your Children

America was told to me once as a story about a
banquet and barbarians,
coupled with cornbread and colonization and
dubbed thanksgiving.
Essentially a euphemism
for the feast that
generated a genocide.
Hyperbole has warped this holiday
into pumpkin pie and ice cream instead of history.
Justified the lies because of
kindness and kids.
Let them learn through
mashed potatoes instead of massacres, through
Native Americans with headdresses
Or
Pilgrims squashing
quarrels with handshakes and conversation.
Rewrite the
story and extrapolate morals like
Thanks giving rather than the
unintended consequence and
Veiled prejudice and
Weary alliance. Create
xenial stories woven for the
your kids to validate the
zealots.

Better Life

There is a bomb.
Strapped tight to the center of my chest,
wires twisted to spell out "child of an immigrant."

And the clock,
getting louder with my every passing moment,
is ticking to the tune of high expectation.

My parents blew up their lives for this,
crossed oceans and made roots of mountains,
so I could have rolling hills of opportunity and options.

And yet, gratitude tangles with anxiety
as this bomb of a better life counts down the clock,
bringing me closer to the explosion of my inevitable disappointment.

Patricia Nwoko

Patriot

I pledge allegiance
Seated and silent
And squirm under the weight of nationalism mixing with a dozen

students

And I stare at this flag
Of a republic divided
By class and race and opinion

And this nation of a god I don't think I believe in
And of justice and liberty
And a part of me finds it as unbelievable as an omnipotent deity

And people are staring, briefly,
The flicker of their eyes ask me what I am doing
And, seated,

I want to say gratitude and pride are layered like stripes,
Dividing citizens into red and white
And somewhere, a little past pride, hubris lays waiting,

I want to say this sitting reminds me of my chosen side,
But instead, I stay silent while they recite their pride,
As though a classroom is the stage for my rebellion

They ask me, with a couple arrant stares, what I am saying
by sitting and staying quiet
And I tell them I am saying that

This pride feels a little like arrogance
And that hubris is a fatal flaw for a reason
They call me ungrateful

So quick to tell me to go back to where I came from
As if this isn't also my flag and my god and my country

Security

there are two exits in this theater
and maybe the guy in the back has a gun
or maybe he is just alone
and maybe his hands are just in his pockets, bulging,
or maybe he will be desperate for attention and angry
and maybe he will use bullets to talk to me
or maybe i will take the second exit, the one by the steps,
and maybe he will spare me because of my smile when he held the door open
or maybe the fancy heated seats will make poor defense weapons
and i will not make it
or maybe there will be a different guy with a gun
and maybe he will save us by fighting bullet with bullet
or maybe if there weren't so many goddamn guns
I wouldn't be so damn scared before watching Ballads

or maybe he is just fidgety and anxious

there are two exits in the cafeteria
and maybe the guy behind me has a gun in his backpack—

Army Brat

They told me you died for this,
for me,
though i think it was a strange way of saying
this country.
They told me your blood flowed,
red and white and army green,
but honestly I just picture it flowing.
I imagine the maggots picking
at the gunpowder staining your hands,
I imagine them bloody.

You used to say,
I had a penchant for imagining,

I imagined the war to be a necessary thing
until they shipped the pieces of you
back to me.
I imagine now,
that you died for something more,
if not peace,
maybe then
for me.

Midnight Oil

burn me,
start at the wick,
where I am still hopeful and happy,
and burn me down,
melt me into demotivation and domestic agony,
burn me until
I am ashes of the person I used to be,
the person who used to love and laugh and spend time with family,
take the ashes left behind and burn them,
burn me into embers
until I am gone completely

Patricia Nwoko

The Day We Stopped Running

was more inconsequential than I thought.
I thought it would be this loud, catastrophic thing.
That maybe our feet,
outrunning the big bad World collapsing,
were keeping the Earth turning.
I thought, we were Atlas,
But, we never had the World on our shoulders
maybe only Grecian hubris
and an impending tragedy.

The day we stopped running,
was a forgetting rather than an acting.
It was the day George Floyd
stopped making rounds through our heads and
media circuits.
It was the day we started drinking Starbucks again
and kept investing in JP Morgan
and supporting the Kanye Wests.

The day we stopped running,
we shed our self-righteousness and performative conscious,
like it was a fashion trend.
We forgot about the World closing in,
Stopped being suffocated by change and
social justice.

The day we stopped running
happened as quickly as we'd started.
I remember us running,
but I can't really remember the reason,
but I'm not even sure if we cared all the much about it
to begin with.

The day we stopped running
happened long before we started.

Blue Moose

There is life in this cafe,
or rather there is art,
or maybe I don't know the difference.
But, regardless, it surrounds me here.
In the orangish light and the music
being strummed by an older man
who writes his own lyrics
about life and love and little moments.
And it is a Wednesday and I feel the type of alive
that makes you feel like there is a chance you will never die.
Maybe art doesn't.
Maybe you can't retire from this.
Because art lives in humans
the way humans use art to live.
We like to discredit it.
The merits of artists and art.
Because the world need engineers and mechanics
And it does.
But when I leave,
the night air feels a little more potent,
and I am certain that there is life in this world,
and that there is art,
and that there is no difference.
And I think that we also need this.

Patricia Nwoko

When the Sun Doesn't Rise

there will be prayer
by mega-church pastors
who spent millions on private air-fare
and they will tell you
that maybe a donation will make the sun resurface.
they will tell you
that maybe money will pay your ticket to the heavens.
and in the darkness they will keep themselves warm
by lining their pockets.

and there will be advice.
sympathetic advertisements
from billion-dollar corporations
who will try to sell you heat,
as if they are selling you kindness and salvation
and they will hope you forget
the way they turned the pressure cooker
up for this planet.

and there will be escape,
on rocket ships
built for people outside our tax brackets
and it will fly the elites somewhere far
with water and sunshine and beaches
and they will wave their goodbyes
from the windows as they pass
as if this is shocking,
as if the rocket ships weren't the issue
to begin with.

when the sun doesn't rise,
it won't be us,
free of private jets and billion-dollar fossil fuel investment,
Mother Nature will be punishing,
and yet,
it will not be them
left to face their consequences
when the sun doesn't rise again.

Patricia Nwoko

Euthanasia

Sometimes I wish we could help them,
the way we help stray dogs
or rabid things.
Put a bullet in its temple
and put it out of its misery.
It would be kinder
than to let them exist,
scrounging on their own,
a pathetic attempt at surviving.
It is a kindness
to lose the park benches
for them to sleep
and the places for them to eat.
Because if we are honest,
it's a little unsightly.
I say, we clean up the streets,
it's only humane.
Killing the homeless slowly.

The American Dream

was never made for me.
And even in its creation,
a sleepy idea,
a bedtime story to tell children
about little boys pulling themselves up
with the help of daddy's money,
it was hard to believe.
Maybe there is something deceitful
about the idea of a meritocracy,
maybe the world wasn't meant
for people like me to succeed.
Maybe these rose colored glasses
they call a dream
were meant to keep me passive,
lethargic in the face of this system
fighting to keep me stationary.
But, I am tired of day-dreaming
through life
and being asked to forget
the American reality.

The American Dream
was never made for me,
but I will not be held back
by a melancholy ideology.

Patricia Nwoko

About the author

Patricia Nwoko is a Nigerian-American who was born in Morgantown, WV. She has been reading and writing for as long as she can remember. But it wasn't until Sophomore year of high school where she started to really get into sharing her writing. She shared a lot of her work to her school's literary magazine and auditioned for West Virginia's Governor's School of the Arts for writing and she got in. There, she delved into poetry and discovered her love for it. The summer going into and all throughout Junior year, she cultivated her poetry and submitted to the William F. DeVault/Venetian Spider Press poetry contest.

She won a publishing deal for a poetry collection which has helped her cultivate a voice in her poetry. She is now 18 and strives to talk about different junctures of her identity like womanhood, race, and American inequality. She shares her poetry at open mic nights and talent competitions and submits to literary magazines across the internet.

In 2024 it was announced that her book Uniquely Unspecial would be nominated for the 2025 Maya Angelou Book Award.